W9-ANK-278

Contents

1. Bartlett Pond 4

2. Sunken Treasure 18

3. Mrs. Locket 26

4. The Blue China Teapot 31

5. "Gordon, Stand Still!" 38

6. The Shark's Mom 47

1

Bartlett Pond

This story is about a club called Beagle and Co. Beagle's full name is Daniel Beagle. He looks a little like a hound dog, with floppy hair and a long nose. It's just the right size, his dad says, for poking into other people's business.

His best friend is Jamal, sometimes known as Jam.

The Case of the Smiling Shark

TESSA KRAILING

Illustrated by Jan Lewis

PACIFIC
LEARNING

© 2001 Pacific Learning
© 1996 Written by **Tessa Krailing**
Illustrated by **Jan Lewis**
US Edit by **Alison Auch**

This Americanized Edition of *The Case of the Smiling
Shark*, originally published in English in 1996, is
published by arrangement with Oxford University
Press.

05 04 03 02 01
10 9 8 7 6 5 4 3 2 1

Published by
   Pacific Learning
   P.O. Box 2723
   Huntington Beach, CA 92647-0723
   www.pacificlearning.com

ISBN: 1-59055-026-9
PL-7401

Jamal is a math wizard and carries a calculator everywhere. He's always using it to figure things out. He even calculated how many times their teacher, Ms. Olesky, says, "Honestly, class, you're the absolute limit!"

Jamal reckons it must be at least six times a day. That is thirty times a week, which is one thousand, two hundred times a year, not counting weekends and holidays.

The third member of the club is Wesley Clark. He doesn't have a nickname. Everyone agrees that being named Wesley must be bad luck enough. Wesley was born unlucky. If a meteorite fell out of the sky onto just one person in the whole wide world, you can bet it would fall on Wesley.

Marietta is the fourth member of Beagle's club. The rest of the club sometimes try to leave her behind. Usually, though, they let her come along. This is because – even though they don't like to admit it – she's the bravest. This is useful when the club finds itself in a dangerous situation.

One of their main adventures happened the time Ms. Olesky asked for volunteers to help clean up the litter in Bartlett Pond.

That day, poor Wesley was even unluckier than usual...

Their whole adventure started innocently enough.

"Bartlett Pond is a disgrace," Ms. Olesky told the class one Friday afternoon. "Now, who'd like to come and help me clean it up tomorrow morning?"

Not one single person raised a hand.

"Honestly, class, you're the absolute limit!" Ms. Olesky exclaimed. "This is your chance to do something for the community. Surely there's someone who'd like to help?"

Beagle shifted uncomfortably in his seat. Ms. Olesky could be a very convincing person.

She just stood there and stared at the class. Beagle knew that no one was going anywhere until Ms. Olesky had her volunteers.

He had to do something so the class could go home for the weekend.

He raised his hand. "We'll do it," he said. "Jamal and Wesley and I, we'll help you clean up the pond."

"Excellent!" Ms. Olesky beamed at all three of them. "Meet me Bartlett Park at ten o'clock sharp – and wear your boots and oldest clothes."

On Saturday morning, Beagle was the first to arrive. Bartlett Park was large and overgrown, and surrounded by houses.

The pond was at one end of the park. It was shaped like a banana and curved around a clump of trees. Beagle dipped the toe of his boot in the thick white scum lying around the edge. Ms. Olesky was right, the pond was in terrible shape. It was going to take a lot of work.

Then Jamal arrived. "I don't know why you told Ms. Olesky we'd help, Beagle," he grumbled.

I can think of a lot of things I'd rather do on a Saturday morning than clean up a disgusting pond.

Wesley was the next to arrive. The other two stared at him.

"Wesley, didn't you hear Ms. Olesky tell us to wear our oldest clothes?" Beagle asked.

"I know, I know, but I'm doing something special for the community," said Wesley.

You know how my grandparents make me dress up for every "event"!

Wesley had no mother or father, so he lived with his grandparents. They were older than most people's grandparents, and they had some old-fashioned ideas about life.

At that moment Ms. Olesky came jogging up in a red warm-up suit.

"Good, you're on time. Any questions before we begin?"

"Just one," said Beagle. "What if we find something cool that was thrown away, like an old football? Can we keep it?"

"I don't see why not," said Ms. Olesky. "Okay, kids, let's get started. You tackle this end. I'll get going on the other." She jogged off around the clump of trees until she was out of sight.

For a while they worked in silence, pulling out all kinds of trash from soggy cardboard boxes to empty soda cans. They passed them back to Wesley, who was keeping as far away from the pond as possible.

Suddenly Marietta came flying up. "There you are! I've been looking for you everywhere. What are you guys doing?"

"We're cleaning out the pond," said Beagle.

"I'll help you," said Marietta.

She pulled on an extra pair of boots that Ms. Olesky had brought and leaned over where the water was deepest. It was brown and murky and full of strange ploppings and gurglings.

"I'll bet there are sharks in there," she said.

"The chances of finding a shark in that pond," Jamal said, doing a quick calculation in his head, "are about one in sixty-five million."

At that exact moment a huge and menacing shadow darkened the surface of the pond.

"There's one!" exclaimed Marietta. The others stared into the water. Sure enough, staring right back at them was a shark's face with rows of pointed teeth and mean little eyes.

It was smiling!

2

Sunken Treasure

"Are you kids looking for something?"

The voice didn't come from the pond. It came from behind them.

Beagle and Co. turned to see the shark standing on the bank, smiling toothily. It wasn't really a shark, of course. It was a man with sharklike teeth and greasy hair.

It must have been his reflection they'd seen in the water.

"We're cleaning out the pond," Beagle told him.

"Is that so?" He smiled even wider. "Then I reckon I'll hang around for a while to see if you find something interesting."

He propped his back against a tree. Marietta looked at him scornfully. "You could *help* us, you know."

That wasn't easy. As they worked,
Beagle could feel the shark man's
mean little eyes watching them.

"What do you think he wants, Jam?"
he whispered.

"I don't know," Jamal whispered back to him.

Wesley had been getting closer and closer to the edge of the pond. Just then, he reached out to grab a piece of floating cardboard and lost his balance.

"Oh, noooo!" he shouted, waving his arms around like a windmill. "I think... I'm going... to... to..."

SPLASH

Luckily, the pond was shallow so
Wesley was in no danger of drowning.
When he stood up, his face and hands
were covered in black sludge. Slimy
green algae was clinging to his suit...
and he had a huge grin on his face.

He staggered from the pond, holding
out his hand. Beagle and Jamal saw
what looked like a hunk of mud lying
in Wesley's palm. "What is it?" they
asked together.

"Yeah, what is it, Wesley?" said Marietta. "What did you find?"

"Can't you see?" Wesley wiped off some of the mud to reveal a small, round object with a faint metallic gleam.

"It's a coin!" said Beagle.

"It's a *silver dollar*," said Jamal.

"It's sunken treasure," said Marietta. "Wesley, you're rich!"

Just then a voice spoke behind them. It made them jump.

You kids found something? Something in the pond?

They had forgotten about the shark man. Wesley quickly hid the coin behind his back.

"It's just an old button," said Beagle. "Somebody must have thrown it away."

Nobody moved. Marietta said defiantly, "You can't. It's ours. Go away."

"Hey, that's no way to talk." The shark man's voice was soft and menacing. He loomed over Wesley. "Come on, kid. No more messing around. Show me what you've got in your hand."

3

Mrs. Locket

Suddenly a high, shaky voice called out, "Is he all right? Is he safe?" An old lady came hurrying toward them.

Wesley groaned. "Oh no, it's Mrs. Locket, my grandmother's best friend."

Mrs. Locket arrived, breathless. "I was looking out of my window just as that poor boy fell into the water."

She peered into Wesley's face. "My word, it's Wesley Clark – and in your best suit too!"

Wesley was still clutching his precious coin. He looked down at his jacket, which was covered in slimy pond scum. "Um, I don't know…"

"She'll have a fit when she sees you." Mrs. Locket clucked her tongue and shook her head.

You'd better come home with me so we can get you cleaned up.

Then she dragged poor Wesley across the park to her house.

The other kids looked around for the shark man.

"He's gone!" said Beagle.

"He must have run off when he saw Mrs. Locket," said Jamal.

"What a coward," said Marietta. "Imagine being scared of a sweet little old lady!"

"We'd better get back to cleaning the pond," said Beagle.

Wait a second.

Jamal looked thoughtful. "What if – and that's a big if – Marietta was right about the sunken treasure? I mean, Wesley only found one coin."

Beagle's eyes gleamed. "You think there might be more?"

"It's possible, and Ms. Olesky definitely said we could keep anything we found."

"That means we'll *all* be rich," said Marietta, and she waded into the pond, right up to the top of her boots.

4

The Blue China Teapot

Meanwhile Wesley was cleaning up under Mrs. Locket's watchful eye. She stood by while he scrubbed his face and hands. Then she took his jacket into the yard to remove the pond slime.

While she was gone Wesley washed the mud off the silver dollar and slipped it into his pants pocket.

When Mrs. Locket came back she handed him his jacket. "Here you are, Wesley. It's the best I could do. Now how on earth did you manage to fall into the water?"

Wesley shrugged. "It's because I'm unlucky, I guess." He touched the coin in his pocket. "At least, I usually am."

Mrs. Locket sighed. "I've been unlucky too. Yesterday a young man came to the door and offered to dig up my garden. I agreed because my back's been bad lately and digging is such hard work.

"When he finished I asked him in for a nice cup of tea. The next thing I knew, he'd run off with my teapot!"

Maybe he was thirsty...

"Oh, he didn't take the old brown teapot I use for making tea. No, he took my special blue china teapot – the one I keep my special money in.

"Of course I ran after him. I chased him halfway across the park, as far as the pond. Then I lost him." Mrs. Locket's lip started to tremble.

"Did you tell the police, Mrs. Locket?" Wesley asked.

"Of course. I told them exactly what he looked like. He had mean little eyes – and pointed teeth."

Wesley stared at her.

"In fact, they were exactly like a shark. Still, I don't suppose they'll ever find him. When I think of him getting away with my blue teapot I could – I could – " Mrs. Locket looked very fierce. "Why, I could just *scream!*"

"Maybe he didn't get away with it. Maybe he dropped it when you ran after him." Again Wesley touched the coin in his pocket.

"Mrs. Locket, this money you had in the blue china teapot – was it bills or coins?"

Coins – more than sixty silver dollars.

"I'd had them for years," continued Mrs. Locket. "They belonged to my mother." She wiped her eyes with her handkerchief. "Now I'll never see them again."

Wesley sighed.

Somehow he'd known it was too good to be true. He took his hand out of his pocket and gave the coin to Mrs. Locket.

"Here's one of them," he said, "and I think I know where we can find the rest."

5

"Gordon, Stand Still!"

"I found something!" Marietta fished a brownish-blue object out of the water. "It's hard – and round – and it a has a spout at one end."

"Aw, Marietta, it's just a dirty old teapot," said Jamal. He was on his stomach, gazing into the pond. "We are looking for treasure, remember?"

Marietta scrambled out of the water and showed the teapot to Beagle. "It feels heavy... and listen."

She shook it. It made a rattling noise. "It sounds as if it's filled with little stones."

Beagle looked into the teapot.

I don't think they're stones. I think they're...

Before he could finish, a large hand swooped down and tried to grab the teapot from Marietta. "That's mine," growled the shark man, appearing from the bushes.

Give it
to me!

No!

Marietta held it tightly. "It's not yours, it's mine. Go away, you big mean bully."

"She's right," said Beagle. "Ms. Olesky said we could keep anything we found. So it's our teapot. We found it, not you."

"Well, now you've lost it!" The shark man pulled the teapot out of Marietta's hands and ran off with it.

At the same moment Wesley and Mrs. Locket came hurrying across the park. "There he is!" cried Mrs. Locket. "That's the man. Stop, thief!"

The shark man heard her voice and glanced over his shoulder.

He didn't see Jamal's stretched-out legs. He tripped and fell with a thud.

The teapot flew through the air. It landed on the hard ground and smashed to pieces, its contents scattering everywhere.

Jamal sat up to take a closer look. "Hey, those aren't stones!" he said. "They're..."

"Silver dollars!" Wesley arrived, panting. "That man stole them from Mrs. Locket. Quick, stop him!"

The shark man jumped to his feet and took off like a rocket around the clump of trees.

That's when he came face to face with Ms. Olesky.

"Gordon Fowler!" she exclaimed. "What on earth are you doing here?"

She looked over his shoulder. There was Mrs. Locket shaking her fist, and Jamal rubbing his leg that had just been tripped over.

"It appears that you're still causing trouble," she continued sternly. "You haven't changed since you were in my class ten years ago."

The shark man, a.k.a. Gordon Fowler, started to back away. At that moment Ms. Olesky snapped, "Gordon, *stand still!*"

Amazingly, he did.

"Now, will somebody please tell me what's going on?"

Everyone spoke at once.

Somehow Ms. Olesky managed to make sense of it all. "Honestly, Gordon, you're the absolute limit," she said.

Well, I'm afraid we'll have to call the police.

6

The Shark's Mom

The shark man looked scared. "No, please – don't call the police. My mom will be furious if she finds out."

"Ah, yes, I remember your mom," Ms. Olesky said. "I can imagine just how furious she's going to be. I'm afraid you should have thought of that before you stole Mrs. Locket's teapot."

"The police are already looking for him," said Wesley. "Mrs. Locket told them what he looks like."

"Yes, I did," said Mrs. Locket. "I told them he had greasy hair and mean little eyes."

"In that case," said Ms. Olesky, "I guess it won't be long before you're caught, Gordon."

The shark man looked more than scared. He looked terrified.

"Please, Ms. Olesky," he begged. "*Please* don't call the police. I'll do anything you ask."

"That's up to Mrs. Locket." Ms. Olesky turned to the old lady. "What do you think?"

Mrs. Locket looked uncertain. "Well, I suppose... if he promises never to do such a thing again..."

Ms. Olesky turned back to the shark man. "Do you promise?"

He gulped. "I promise."

"All right, Gordon. The first thing you need to do is pick up all those silver dollars lying on the ground. Then give them back to Mrs. Locket. And don't forget to tell her that you're sorry."

The shark man started crawling around in the mud. When he had collected all the coins, he handed them over to the old lady, muttering, "I'm sorry, Mrs. Locket."

Mrs. Locket accepted the coins – and the apology – with a gracious nod of her head.

"Okay," said Ms. Olesky briskly. "Now, I want you to go down to the mall. You can buy her a brand-new teapot to replace the one you broke. Do you understand?"

Yes, Ms. Olesky.

He sounded timid and scared – not at all like a shark

"Well, hurry up! What are you waiting for?"

"Nothing, Ms. Olesky. I'm going, Ms. Olesky."

He hurried off across the park as if a police dog were already panting at his heels.

Ms. Olesky waited until he had disappeared before turning to Wesley.

"As for you, Wesley," she said with a sigh, "I think you'd better go straight home and get yourself cleaned up."

Wesley groaned. "My grandmother will be furious," he muttered.

Mrs. Locket continued, "Because I will come with you. I'll tell her how you helped me get my money back. She can't possibly be mad at you then. In fact, I want you to have some kind of a reward. How about the biggest ice-cream sundae you've ever seen?"

Wesley grinned from ear to ear. "Can it be vanilla with chocolate sauce?"

"Whatever you want."

Wesley's eyes lit up. It looked as if he were finally having some *good* luck.

When they were gone, Jamal said, "Imagine – the shark man went to our school ten years ago."

"He must have been as mean and nasty then as he is now," said Marietta. "He sure is scared of his mom, though, isn't he?"

"If his mom is the Mrs. Fowler who lives on Washington Street, I'm not surprised," said Jamal. "She's as big as a rhinoceros and at least twice as scary."

"Poor Gordon," Marietta sighed. "I almost feel sorry for him, living in the same house as a rhino – even if he *is* a shark."

Beagle grinned.

One thing's for sure. Seeing Ms. Olesky again definitely took the smile off his face!

About the Author

I wrote my first story when
I was four years old.
From that moment I
knew I wanted to be a
writer, but it was many
years before my first
book (which was
about dinosaurs) was
published. Since then,
I have written over thirty
books for children of all ages. Most of all,
I love writing mystery stories and stories
that make people laugh.

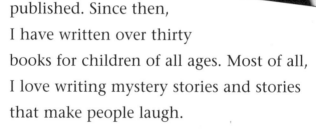

I got the idea for this story while helping
to clean out a pond near my house.

Tessa Krailing